ruth & esther

A DOUBLE-EDGED BIBLE STUDY

ruth & esther

A DOUBLE-EDGED BIBLE STUDY

TH1NK: **Life**Change™

TH1NK
P.O. Box 35001
Colorado Springs, Colorado 80935

www.navpress.com

TH1NK is an imprint of NavPress.

TH1NK and the TH1NK logo are registered trademarks of NavPress. Absence of ® in connection with marks of NavPress or other parties does not indicate an absence of registration of those marks.

ISBN 1-57683-852-8

Cover design by Arvid Wallen

Creative Team: Gabe Filkey s.c.m., Nicci Jordan, Melanie Knox, Steve Parolini, Arvid Wallen, Kathy Mosier, Glynese Northam

Printed in the United States of America

3 4 5 6 7 8 9 10 / 09 08 07

contents

introduction to TH1NK: LifeChange

Double-Edged and Ready for Action

For the word of God is living and active. Sharper than any double-edged sword, it penetrates even to dividing soul and spirit, joints and marrow; it judges the thoughts and attitudes of the heart.

Hebrews 4:12

a reason to study

Studying the Bible is more than homework. It is more than reading a textbook. And it is more than an opportunity for a social gathering. Like Hebrews suggests, the Bible knows us, challenges us, and, yes, judges us. Like a double-edged sword, it's sharp enough to cut through our layers of insecurity and pretense to change our lives forever.

Deep down, isn't that what we want—to actually *experience* God's power in our lives through Scripture? That's what TH1NK: LifeChange is all about. The purpose of this Bible study is to connect you intimately with God's Word. It can change you, not only intellectually but also spiritually, emotionally, maybe even physically. God's Word is that powerful.

The psalmist wrote,

What you say goes, GOD,
*   and stays, as permanent as the heavens.*
Your truth never goes out of fashion;
*   it's as up-to-date as the earth when the sun*
*   comes up. . . .*
If your revelation hadn't delighted me so,
*   I would have given up when the hard times came.*
But I'll never forget the advice you gave me;
*   you saved my life with those wise words.*
Save me! I'm all yours.
*   I look high and low for your words of wisdom.*
The wicked lie in ambush to destroy me,
*   but I'm only concerned with your plans for me.*
I see the limits to everything human,
*   but the horizons can't contain your commands!*

(PSALM 119:89-90,92-96, MSG)

Do you notice the intimate connection the psalmist has with God *because* of the greatness of the Word? He trusts God, he loves Him, and his greatest desire is to obey Him. But the only way he knows how to do any of this is because he knows God's voice, God's words.

the details

Each TH1NK: LifeChange study covers one book of the Bible so you can concentrate on its particular, essential details. Although every study covers a different book (in this case, two books), there are common threads throughout the series. Each study will do the following:

1. Help you understand the book you're studying so well that it affects your daily thinking
2. Teach valuable Bible study skills you can use on your own to go even deeper into God's Word
3. Provide a contextual understanding of the book, offering historical background, word definitions, and explanatory notes
4. Allow you to understand the message of the book as a whole
5. Demonstrate how God's Word can transform you into a bona fide representative of Jesus

Every week, plan on spending about thirty to forty-five minutes on your own to complete the study. Then get together with your group. Depending on the amount of time it takes, you can either go through a whole or a half lesson each week. If you do one lesson per week, you'll finish the study in two and a half months. But it's all up to you.

the structure

The ten lessons include the following elements:

Study. First you'll study the book by yourself. This is where you'll answer questions, learn cultural and biographical information, and ask God some questions of your own.

Live. After you've absorbed the information, you'll want to look in a mirror–figuratively, that is. Think about your life in the context of what you've learned. This is a time to be honest with yourself and with God about who you are and how you are living.

Connect. You know that a small-group study time isn't just for hanging out and drinking soda. A small group provides accountability and support. It's one thing to say to yourself, *I'm really going to work on this* and entirely another thing to say it to a group of your friends. Your friends can support your decisions, encourage you to follow through, and pray for you regularly. And vice versa.

In your group, you'll want to talk with each other about things you discovered on your own, things that went unanswered, things that challenged you, and things that changed you. Use the guidance in this section to lead your discussion. After that, pray for each other.

Go deeper. Thirsty for more? Just can't get enough? Then use the guidance in this section to explore even deeper the vastness of Scripture. It's similar to extra credit for all you overachievers who love to learn.

Memory verse of the week. Did a particular verse make you think? Is there a verse you can't get out of your head? Write it down and memorize it. Allow God's Word to permanently brand itself in your head and your heart.

Notes. At the end of each chapter, there are some pages for notes. Use them to ask questions of God or yourself, to write important verses and observations, or anything else you want to jot down.

now go!

You are now ready to experience God and the Bible in an intense, new way. So jump in headfirst. Allow the double-edged sword of Scripture to pierce your mind, your heart, your life.

Introduction to Ruth

selfless love

Most of us from time to time find it difficult to believe that our lives are significant. We go through the motions day after day, straining to see how our lives matter. *There's nothing much to it. My life is boring. I doubt sitting on the couch watching MTV all day will change the course of history.* It's easy to think that way in the moment, but our lives have the potential to make a difference – a life-changing difference–even if we don't get to see it during our lifetime.

Such is the case for our heroine, Ruth. At first glance, the story of Ruth seems to come out of nowhere. It's placed between Judges–a book of unruly people, unfit leaders, violence, murder, and rape–and 1 Samuel–a book about some of the most well-known people in biblical history (perhaps you've heard of King David?). Ruth, on the other hand, is a brief story (only four chapters) of some noncelebrities–an old widow and a young widow–trying to figure out how to live their everyday lives. After Ruth's husband dies, she and her widowed mother-in-law are left penniless, so she finds a way to make a living by getting married again. Um . . . yeah. Just doesn't stand out as a monumentally captivating story, does it?

Ah, but that's not the whole story. Without Ruth, our Savior, Jesus, would never have been born. During the next few chapters, you'll encounter this plain Jane, an unlikely link in the lineage of Jesus—an unlikely link who made a huge difference.

map of Israel under the judges

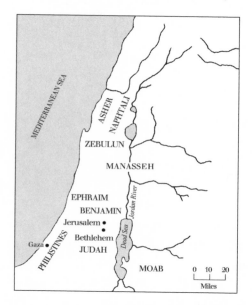

timeline for the book of Ruth

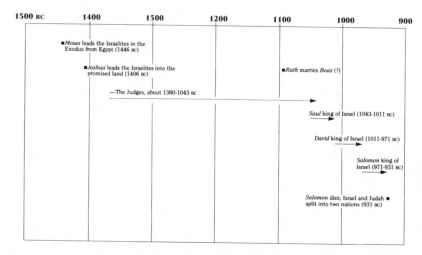

some history

The story of Ruth was a breath of fresh air for Israel. It happened before they chose their first king, Saul. Many people see it as a story of selfless love—and it is—but it's also a reminder that God can bring His will about even when His people ignore Him.

So here's how it goes. After Moses died, Joshua's job was to lead the Israelites into the Promised Land and either kill the Canaanites (the people who were already living there) or enslave them so they wouldn't entice Israel to join in their pagan behaviors and rituals. But that's not how it happened. Instead, the Israelites decided to do business with the Canaanites and even intermarry with them.

God had promised the Israelites He'd give them sure victory over Canaan if they remained faithful to Him. He also promised, however, that they'd be defeated if they gave their loyalties to other gods. So what was the end result of their disobedience? A repeating cycle of apostasy (rejecting God), inevitable oppression by foreign peoples, remembering God and begging for His help, and receiving His merciful deliverance.

Many times throughout the book of Judges it says, "In those days Israel had no king; everyone did as he saw fit" (Judges 17:6, for example). While there were no kings, there were judges. Judges were endowed by God with special skills to lead the tribes. They were leaders in warfare, but they were also wise, discerning, and moral. If the judges defeated an enemy, there was peace in their region for a generation. The Israelites respected them, and sometimes the judges could even convert some of the Israelites to God's ways. But there was no logic to the structure of their government. No judge ever governed more than a few of the twelve tribes of Israel. And while there may have been peace in one or a few of the tribes, other tribes still practiced pagan activities, such as child sacrifice and prostitution.

Judah, the tribe of Israel from which Jesus would come, is the setting for Ruth's story. Interestingly, Judah is rarely mentioned in the book of Judges. In fact, no judge over Judah is ever named, nor is any battle for liberation described. Judges does tell us, however, that during the time of Samson, the Philistines dominated Judah, and the tribe accepted its foreign rulers. One village referenced in the book of Ruth—Bethlehem—showed no signs of war or Philistine influence; it was like a safe island in a sea of violence and immorality.

We have an approximate idea of when Ruth lived. Her great-grandson David (yes, *that* David) began his rule in Judah in 1011 BC at the age of thirty, so Ruth and Boaz probably married sometime between 1100 and 1075 BC.

the state of the monarchy

Because Ruth 4:22 mentions David, we know that it must have been written sometime after he became king of Israel. In his lifetime (and his son Solomon's), Israel finally defeated the Canaanites and attained the peace and prosperity Moses promised. (If only they would have obeyed God in the first place . . . How many of us have said *that?*) After Solomon left his position as king, most of Israel gave up on the royal house of David, but Judah stayed faithful, continuing to adore him and crown his descendants. No matter what happened in Israel, Judah looked back to David's throne as a golden age.

The book of Ruth, then, was likely written by someone who revered David, but really, it could have been anyone who lived after 1000 BC. Because of the literary style of the book, most scholars agree that it was written between 1000 and 600 BC while Judah was still ruled by kings from David's line. But the story itself is probably a tradition passed down in Ruth and David's family because the tale so vividly reflects their customs.

the girl from out of town

The author continually reminds us that Ruth was from Moab and therefore was not an Israelite. That reminder is important because

Israel considered Moab an inferior people descended from an incestuous union (see Genesis 19:30-38). And further, Moses' law stated, "No Ammonite or Moabite or any of his descendants may enter the assembly of the LORD, even down to the tenth generation" (Deuteronomy 23:3) because Ammon and Moab had consistently been hostile toward Israel.

Because of Moab's sordid past and relationship with Israel and because of the law in Deuteronomy, which makes it clear that Moabites aren't permitted to be God's people, it seems odd (astonishing, actually) that God chose a Moabitess to be the ancestor of both David and Jesus. Likewise, it's odd that the author unabashedly stressed Ruth's identity and that Jews throughout history have revered Ruth enough to acknowledge her story as Scripture.

In light of the law in Deuteronomy 23:3, why was David allowed to be not only a member of the congregation of Israel but also a king? It's true that the Israelites of Ruth's day were casual toward God's law, but why did *God* select this family above all others? As you study the book of Ruth, keep these questions in mind. And on that note, let's move on to the lessons.

first impressions

Lesson 1

May the LORD deal with me,
be it ever so severely, if anything but death separates you
and me.

Ruth 1:17

For most women, putting on makeup is a formulaic, everyday occurrence (except on the frumpy days). Some start with foundation; some don't. Next they add powder, blush, eye shadow, mascara, lipstick, and whatever else the routine requires. When a woman is finished, she looks at her whole face and evaluates her artwork. She judges how she looks by the whole of her made-up face, not by the individual elements (although it really is annoying when the mascara clumps up).

That's the way to read the book of Ruth. It's put together in what seems like a formulaic, everyday manner—just like makeup. Putting on mascara or blush doesn't take much creativity, but the end product is often a work of art. Similarly, the best way to study Ruth is not to dissect it into individual elements but to appreciate it as a whole. That doesn't mean the individual elements aren't crucial to understanding the story; it just means that before you can appreciate the complexities of the book, you've got to know the big picture.

If you haven't already, read the introduction on pages 13–17. This will introduce you to Ruth and show you how the book fits into God's great story. Then, read the book of Ruth twice (it's only four chapters, so don't panic). First, try reading a literal translation such as the ESV (English Standard Version) or the NASB (New American Standard Bible). Then consider reading a paraphrase such as *The Message.* That way, you will connect with both the *literal meaning* and the *feelings* of the text.

study

As you're reading, think about the different elements of story found in the book, such as the plot, the main characters, any recurring themes, and the author's purpose. What is the author trying to explain, convince us of, or encourage us to do or accomplish?

1 Write your comments about the following:

Important repeated words and/or phrases

Key ideas and themes

Things that puzzle or surprise you

2 Write your first impressions about the following characters:

Naomi

Ruth

Orpah

Boaz

The unnamed kinsman in chapter 4

3 After these first two readings, what do you think are the main themes or purposes of Ruth?

4 How does Ruth's story affect your ideas about God? What does the story tell you about Him?

live

5   Can you already see lessons this book might teach you? What are they?

connect

Talk with your group about your hopes and expectations for this study. Have someone write them down so that as you go through the study, your leader can remind you of your goals and help you hold each other accountable. Then pray together, asking God to lead your group to a deeper understanding of Him through these incredible women of Scripture.

go deeper

For further study, read a commentary about Ruth to get additional perspective on the book. Try *Matthew Henry's Commentary on the Whole Bible, Complete and Unabridged* or *Thru the Bible.*

memory verse of the week

Did a particular verse make you think? Is there a verse you can't get out of your head? Write it down and memorize it. Allow God's Word to permanently brand itself in your head and your heart.

notes from group discussion

questioning God

Lesson 2

I went away full, but the LORD has brought me back empty. Why call me Naomi? The LORD has afflicted me; the Almighty has brought misfortune upon me.

Ruth 1:21

During Asia's tsunami crisis in December 2004, many people were asking, "Is God really good? Because it seems as if all He's doing is killing hundreds of thousands of people and ruining the lives of others." That's a good question to ask. During crises, whether large-scale like the tsunami or smaller-scale like a breakup, we *should* ask that question. God wants us to question Him; He knows that if we do, our trust in Him will only grow stronger.

Naomi took a step beyond questioning God by claiming that He was actually against her. With heartfelt emotion, she cried out, "The Almighty has made my life very bitter" (1:20). Have you ever felt that way? As you read this section of Ruth's story, put yourself first in Naomi's shoes and then in Ruth's.

Read Ruth 1:1-22.

study

fyi

- *Famine (1:1).* Obviously, rainfall is a pretty unpredictable thing, and it was during Ruth's day as well. Israel relied on rain for their crops, and drought and famine were common. But because of unusual wind patterns, there could be a famine in Judah and plenty of rain just across the Dead Sea in Moab (see map on page 14).[1]

- *Bethlehem in Judah (1:1).* Beth-lechem means "house of bread"—a reference to the land's fertility for grain crops.[2] Olives and grapes were northern Israel's main produce, but Judah was a region of wheat and barley farmers. The House of Bread was empty, however, and that's why Naomi and her family left for Moab.

- *Ephrathites (1:2).* Ephrath was the old name for Bethlehem, and people from the surrounding region retained it. The name may also have been used to distinguish established families from newer ones.[3]

- *Sons . . . husband (1:5).* Some people balk at the cause of feminists, sometimes for good reason, but without them, women might still be where Ruth and Naomi were. In their culture, a woman's worth and security depended on her family. Women could not work or earn money, nor could they cultivate land without male relatives. A woman's only hope was found in managing her husband's household and bearing children. She needed sons, not daughters, because grown sons could support her if her husband died. Also, bearing sons was a woman's mission in life; barrenness was regarded as a disgrace and a divine curse. Therefore, a childless widow too old to remarry (namely Naomi after her husband and sons died) was considered worthless and was vulnerable to abuse or death.[4]

1   The meaning of a name was very important in Ruth's day. So what do some of the names in this story mean? Elimelech means "God is King," and Naomi means "pleasant, lovely, delightful." Both are Hebrew names. Mahlon means "weak," and Kilion means "annihilation." Both are Canaanite (pagan) names. No one is quite sure what Ruth means in the Moabite language, but it sounds like the Hebrew word for friendship. In 1:20, Naomi renamed herself Mara, which means "bitter." How do these names reflect the themes of the book?

2   How do you react to Naomi's view of God's hand in her life? Do you think she accurately assessed His involvement, or was she missing the point? Explain your answer.

3   How should a Christian respond to the kind of tragedy Naomi experienced? (Optional: Read Psalm 13; 86; 2 Corinthians 1:8-11; 4:7-18; 5:1-10; 12:7-10.)

• *Mother's home (1:8)*. Here's a little woman power for you. **fyi**
Ancient writers usually referred to the father's home, but
this book was written from a woman's point of view. Likewise, it was
unusual to speak of a man as a woman's husband as it does in verse
3: "Now Elimelech, Naomi's husband . . .".[5]

• *Rest (1:9)*. The word rest has two meanings here. First, it's a key
Old Testament idea that includes peace, security, and blessing. God
promised it to Israel if they remained loyal, but by now you know
all about Israel's inconsistent loyalty. The book of Hebrews says that
the kingdom of God is the fulfillment of the long-awaited Sabbath-
rest promised to Israel. (The only time they really experienced this
rest on earth was under Joshua and again briefly under David and
Solomon.) Second, Naomi is speaking about the kind of security and
blessing a woman could have only if she were married. A Hebrew
reader would understand the second, more obvious meaning but
also couldn't miss the allusion to the rest Israel longed for.

• **Sons, who could become your husbands (1:11)**. The Law stated
that if a man died, his brother had to marry the widow in order to
protect her and continue their family name. This is called levirate
marriage from the Latin word levir, which means "brother-in-law."
(As you can see in chapter 4, the levirate was extended to other
members of the family if there were no brothers.)

• *Her people and her gods (1:15)*. In Ruth's time, the tie to family
and ancestral gods was strong, and people naturally feared strangers
and strange gods. So it was natural that Orpah would leave because
she knew her chances of remarriage in Judah (again, her only real
option for survival) were slim to none. Israelites were prejudiced
against foreigners, and the children of a Moabite might even be
barred from the religious congregation. Plus, any Israelite man
would prefer an Israelite virgin to a penniless Moabite widow.

4 What does Ruth's choice tell you about her?

5 How do you react to Orpah's choice? Do you judge her, or can you relate to her? Why?

6 How did Jesus and Paul describe love in the following verses?

Jesus (John 15:13)

Paul (Philippians 2:4)

7 How did Ruth exemplify this kind of love in 1:16-17?

live

8 Do you know anyone who is hurting as Naomi was? If so, how can you show commitment like Ruth's toward that person? What would such commitment cost you?

9 Are there any other aspects of this chapter that speak to you? Write them down and spend some time in prayer about them.

connect

Share with your group the meaning of your name (if you know it). Then, go around the circle and share the name you would give yourself right now according to your life's circumstance (for example, Naomi chose the name "bitter").

go deeper

Use a concordance and any other Bible study resources you have (see the study resources section on page 115 for ideas) to trace the promise of rest in Scripture. What did it mean throughout biblical history, and what does it mean for your life? How can you enter God's rest?

memory verse of the week

Did a particular verse make you think? Is there a verse you can't get out of your head? Write it down and memorize it. Allow God's Word to permanently brand itself in your head and your heart.

notes from group discussion

crazy things

Lesson 3

Ruth approached quietly, uncovered his feet and lay down.

Ruth 3:7

Women do crazy things to attract the man they want to marry. They manipulate situations: "I had no idea you'd be here!" They spend hours in front of the mirror: "Oh, I just threw myself together in, like, five minutes." Sometimes they even pretend to love something he does, hoping for a date: "How weird! I love hunting too!" But of all the desperate attempts for attention (and let's be honest, most are desperate, if not deceitful), Ruth pretty much tops the charts. I mean, have you ever snuck into your potential beau's bedroom and lay at his feet, just waiting for him to notice you? (Um . . . if you have, it might not be best to bring that up in a group setting.)

The cool thing about feminine wiles, though, is that God can accomplish His goals through them. And before you haughtily say, "*in spite* of them," think of Ruth's story. Many women today would exclaim, "Don't take initiative with a man!" And although that may often be good advice, God's ways are not always so cut-and-dry. Just as the Lord sent rain to refill the House of Bread with grain at harvest time, so He ended the famine in Ruth's and Naomi's lives in a most unconventional way.

Read Ruth 2:1–3:18.

study

Barley harvest (1:22). Barley was harvested in late April through early May, and the wheat harvest followed in May and early June. The harvest included these steps: "(1) cutting the ripened standing grain with hand sickles . . . usually done by men; (2) binding the grain into sheaves—usually done by women; (3) gleaning, i.e., gathering stalks of grain left behind . . .; (4) transporting the sheaves to the threshing floor—often by donkey, sometimes by cart . . .; (5) threshing, i.e., loosening the grain from the straw—usually done by the treading of cattle . . . but sometimes by toothed threshing sledges . . . or the wheels of carts . . .; (6) winnowing—done by tossing the grain into the air with winnowing forks . . . so that the wind, which usually came up for a few hours in the afternoon, blew away the straw and chaff . . . leaving the grain at the winnower's feet; (7) sifting the grain . . . to remove any residual foreign matter; (8) bagging for transportation and storage."[1]

1 In Ruth's day, a single woman had few ways to support herself. She could beg, sell herself into slavery or prostitution, look for a husband among eligible men in the village (where pickings were often slim), or seek help from a male relative. Or, during those two months of harvest, she could glean. Ruth chose to glean to support herself and her mother-in-law. What does this tell you about her?

2   In the following verses, what else do you learn about Ruth's character?

   2:7

   2:10,13

Water jars (2:9). Gleaning was hard and dehydrating work, and it took even more work (and lots of time) if a gleaner had to draw her own water. So water was a jealously protected commodity. The law of gleaning didn't require the landowner to provide water, food, or protection from men.

3   Describe what you learn about Boaz's character from the following verses.

   2:4

   2:11-12

   2:8-9,14-16

- *Kinsman-redeemers (2:20).* In Hebrew, this is go'el. It's a **fyi** recurring word in Ruth's story with both a verb and noun meaning. The verb means "to redeem" or "to act as a kinsman." The noun means "kinsman" but implies the duties that went with the blood relationship. The kinsman-redeemer was basically responsible for any leftover duties his deceased relative had left behind or for picking up the pieces resulting from the family's loss, such as providing an heir for a brother who had died, redeeming land, redeeming a relative from slavery, or avenging a murdered relative.

- *Threshing floor (3:3).* This was probably a space of hard, smooth rock or clay in an exposed place downwind of the village. It had to be carefully chosen to catch the afternoon or evening breeze because both threshing and winnowing were done there. After the day's work was done, the men hung around to eat, drink, and dance, but the women went home. And after the men left, the landowner (Boaz in this case) stayed through the night to guard the grain from theft.[2]

- *The meeting at the threshing floor (3:1-18).* In chapter 2, Ruth took the initiative to provide for Naomi by gleaning. Every day during that time, Ruth worked and ate with the hired laborers and watched how Boaz supervised them. Boaz, in turn, was attentive to Ruth's diligent work. They may have even talked with each other occasionally.

4 Ruth praised Boaz for his kindness (the same word used in 1:8). How did Boaz show the kindness of a kinsman-redeemer in 3:10-15?

5 Boaz praised Ruth for her kindness in seeking a middle-aged husband from her late father-in-law's family instead of finding any young man to marry. To whom and how was Ruth showing kindness?

6 What made Ruth and Boaz different from most people in Israel (see Judges 21:25)?

fyi *Uncover his feet and lie down (3:4).* Although this custom is not mentioned anywhere else in ancient writings, the context makes it clear that Ruth was asking Boaz to marry her. And Boaz didn't think she was promiscuous. Garments were often used symbolically. When Ruth asked Boaz to spread the corner of his garment over her, she was proposing marriage.[3] And when Boaz consented to her request (although it doesn't actually say he wrapped his garment over her, their conversation makes it obvious), he was symbolizing the protective rest he would give her as her husband. Though there was nothing culturally unusual about Naomi's instruction and Ruth's behavior, it was risky for Ruth to lie at the feet of a man who had likely been drinking heavily.

live

7   What have you learned about character in this chapter that you want to apply to your own life?

8   Are there any people in your life to whom you specifically desire to show kindness, either in the way Ruth showed kindness to Boaz or the way Boaz demonstrated kindness to Ruth?

9   What steps can you take to begin showing this kindness?

connect

Perhaps people in your group have funny stories about the way they got someone to notice them. Tell your stories and talk about the results. Or perhaps there are some group members who feel confused about their relationships. Discuss how you believe God has worked or can work in those situations.

go deeper

The Bible has many things to say about a woman of noble (excellent, worthy) character. Study the woman of noble character in Proverbs 31. Although she does some things that may be unrealistic in American culture, think about the things she does and the virtues she possesses that can apply to your own life.

memory verse of the week

Did a particular verse make you think? Is there a verse you can't get out of your head? Write it down and memorize it. Allow God's Word to permanently brand itself in your head and your heart.

notes from group discussion

faithfulness through thick and thin

Lesson 4

May the LORD make the woman who is coming into your home like Rachel and Leah, who together built up the house of Israel.

Ruth 4:11

These days, getting married usually requires things like friendship, love, commitment—you know, the easy stuff. But there's also red tape, which, at the very least, means a marriage certificate, someone to officiate the wedding, and witnesses (hence the necessity for an Elvis impersonator and his girl-friends to accompany new lovers at a Vegas wedding).

Because of all the kinsman-redeemer laws, Ruth and Boaz's red tape looked a little different. Instead of hiring an Elvis look-alike and signing a wedding license, they needed to con-duct a family transaction and remove a sandal. (What?!)

In the last chapter of this story, Boaz married Ruth, a penniless widow from Moab. Was she insignificant? A nobody? Boaz must not have thought so. And neither should we, considering that she did become the great-grandmother of King David—*the* man after God's own heart.

Read Ruth 4:1-22.

study

• *Town gate (4:1).* Towns in Ruth's time were crowded
places with tightly packed buildings and no open squares
or forums. Because of that, all town business was done in the open
space in front of the town gate. The city elders (the judges of that
time) and other men were often found there arbitrating disputes
and witnessing legal business transactions, such as marriages.[1]

• *Naomi . . . is selling the piece of land (4:3).* Technically, widows
could not inherit their husband's property and then sell it.[2] But
because Elimelech had no children, brothers, or uncles, the commu-
nity apparently gave Naomi the right to sell the land.[3] Because she
wasn't able to farm it herself, she had to sell it, and buying it was
part of the kinsman-redeemer's obligation to Elimelech. And though
it isn't specifically mentioned in the story, Naomi had obviously at
some point told Boaz about her intent to sell.

• *Endanger my own estate (4:6).* Okay, here is how the whole
estate thing works: If the unnamed kinsman in this story were
to accept his go'el responsibility, he would have to pay for both
Elimelech's land and Mahlon's widow, Ruth. If the kinsman were
able to buy the land without Ruth, then the land would become
part of his estate and he could pass it on to his sons in his name.
But because the kinsman's duty included marrying Ruth, her first
son and the land would be in Mahlon's family name according to
the law. So, the kinsman would have to pay Naomi for the land
and support Ruth and any sons she might have, but none of that
expense would be credited to his estate. In order to fulfill those
duties, the kinsman would therefore have risked having his own
name lost. In addition, he might have endangered his own estate
by marrying a Moabitess; notice that Boaz reminded everyone of
Ruth's origin in verse 5.

1 Think about the choices that Boaz and the unnamed kinsman made in 4:2-10. What do you learn about each man's priority?

The unnamed kinsman

Boaz

2 How was Boaz rewarded for risking his own name and posterity (see Ruth 4:18-22; Matthew 1:5-16)? How would you have acted if you were Boaz?

3 Can you relate the conclusions you drew in the last two questions to your own life? How so?

4 What effect did Ruth and Boaz's marriage have on Naomi (compare 1:5,21 to 4:13-17)?

5 Remember what Naomi thought God was doing in her life at the beginning of this story when she was empty of wealth, family, and status? What part did God play in filling her emptiness (see 2:3,12; 3:11; 4:13)?

6 In question 4 you explained how Ruth and Boaz's marriage affected Naomi. How did their faithfulness affect the following people?

Elimelech and Mahlon (4:10)

The nation of Israel (4:18-22)

7 What does the story of Ruth show about God's responsibility and people's responsibility in working out God's plans?

God's responsibility

People's responsibility

8   Think back to the question at the beginning of our study of Ruth: "In light of the law in Deuteronomy 23:3, why was David allowed to be not only a member of the congregation of Israel but also a king? It's true that the Israelites of Ruth's day were casual toward God's law, but why did *God* select this family above all others?" Read the old covenant law in Deuteronomy 23:3 and the promise of the new covenant in Isaiah 56:3-8. Do you think it's significant that both David and Jesus descended from a Moabitess? Explain your answer.

live

9   The story of Ruth touches on so many topics, but one key theme is faithfulness. Have you ever been in a situation in which you felt emptied like Naomi? And have you ever experienced an obvious display of God's faithfulness in that same situation? How does this affect your response to other situations in your life, whether past, present, or future?

10   How can you apply these insights to your life today? Spend some time praying about the effect God's faithfulness has on your everyday life.

connect

Talk with each other about what God's faithfulness means to you. As you think about this, consider Naomi and Ruth's story and revisit your answers to question 7. Also, consider sharing your answers for questions 9 and 10 with each other. Pray together about life situations in which you need to be reminded of God's faithfulness.

go deeper

In the Bible (and in other resources, if you want), locate the following people in the genealogy of David. Write down their significance either to this story or to future generations after Ruth and Boaz.

Rachel and Leah

Tamar

Perez

Solomon

memory verse of the week

Did a particular verse make you think? Is there a verse you can't get out of your head? Write it down and memorize it. Allow God's Word to permanently brand itself in your head and your heart.

notes from group discussion

a redeemer

May you be richly rewarded
by the LORD, the God of Israel,
under whose wings you have
come to take refuge.

Ruth 2:12

By now, you should be getting the idea that influence and significance go far beyond the limited perspective we have as individuals. Ruth had no idea of the influence she would have—not a clue. Today we don't just know about her, but we are eternally thankful for her bold and loyal character.

What's also interesting to note is that she couldn't have become influential without the help she received from others. First there was Naomi, who loved her and encouraged her to take a step of faith and seek the favor of Boaz. And then there was Boaz, her kinsman-redeemer, who chose to accept Ruth's brave invitation of marriage and serve her and her mother-in-law's family line. Ruth, Naomi, and Boaz all made unselfish decisions that ultimately contributed to humanity's salvation.

As you review the book of Ruth, consider the fact that you are significant and that you have been redeemed.

Review the book of Ruth.

Types. The word *type* is used to refer to an Old Testament
person, object, or event that God designed to foreshadow

something to come in the New Testament, which is called its antitype.
Types are good to use, within limits, to understand the complexities
of God's Scripture and will. It's not good, however, to go overboard
with type/antitype analyses by basing doctrines on them, pressing
them to extreme applications, or using them as a primary meaning
instead of symbolically.

Read Ephesians 5:25-32 and Revelation 21:2,9-10. In what ways
re Boaz and Ruth types of Christ and the church? Also, how do they
epresent God and Israel?

Review how Boaz acted as a kinsman-redeemer toward Ruth.
Vhat did he do?

In what similar ways is Christ our Kinsman-Redeemer?

4 How did Ruth model the way we should act toward Christ (see 2:10,13; 3:9)?

5 Now that you've studied Ruth's story in detail, look back over what you've learned. Think again about the word *kindness*. Write down how Naomi, Ruth, and Boaz showed kindness toward each other.

Naomi

Ruth

Boaz

6 What did you learn about God from this story?

7 In the first lesson, you wrote your first impressions of the story. Have your thoughts changed at all? If so, what do you now think are its main themes and/or purposes?

> **live**

8 What are key lessons you learned from studying this book?

9 Look back at the Live sections in the previous lessons and read the applications you wanted to make.

a Have you noticed any areas in your life (attitudes, thoughts, opinions, behaviors) that have changed because of what you've learned?

b Ask God to show you particular areas of your life where you can grow.

connect

Talk with your group about the concept of a redeemer. Discuss with each other what that word means to you. Think about human redeemers (like Boaz) and the divine Redeemer (Jesus). Have you had any human redeemers in your life? How do they remind you of Jesus?

go deeper

Read the whole story of Ruth again. Look for new revelations. Ask God to continue to reveal His faithfulness as you read.

memory verse of the week

Did a particular verse make you think? Is there a verse you can't get out of your head? Write it down and memorize it. Allow God's Word to permanently brand itself in your head and your heart.

notes from group discussion

Introduction to Esther

strong faith

On a scale of one to ten, how well do you stick up for yourself? How about for your family? For God? Are you an unabashed wimp, a one on the scale, believing that life is better without conflict? Or are you an in-your-face person, a ten, firm in your belief that confrontation is the spice of life?

Let's take it a step further. How well do you stand up for yourself in the face of danger? It's true that any ten on the scale can argue to the death that her outfit is *not* "so five years ago," but what if someone threatened your life? Or what if someone you love were in danger? Would you risk your own life to keep him from harm—even if your death was almost certain?

There are probably a lot more ones and twos than tens when it comes to life-and-death circumstances.

But Esther, the wife of the king of Persia, had to be at least a nine. For her, backing down in the face of danger was not an option. When Haman, the king's right-hand man, called for all Jews living in Persia to be killed (not knowing that Esther was, in fact, a Jew), Esther knew she had some sticking up to do. The fact that her cousin Mordecai was first on the killing docket probably didn't hurt. Knowing that she had to make a life-and-death decision, Esther exclaimed, "If I perish, I perish" (4:16). Words from a brave woman, indeed.

some history

map of the Persian empire

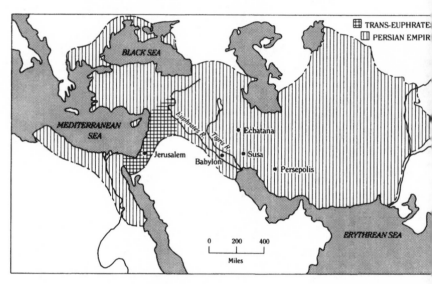

Two centuries after Ruth, Esther plays out her story during one of the "down" seasons of Israel's self-destructive cycle. We know by now that Ruth lived during a time when Israel had no king and everyone "did as he saw fit," which translates, "Everyone made a huge mess of things." Not long after, however, Ruth's great-grandson King David led Israel to a pinnacle of fame, strength, and prosperity. It was a golden time for Israel.

Just another century later, that dream faded when Israel (predictably) plunged back into sin. (But let's not be too quick to judge Israel; it's easy to think of how many times we've rebelled against God.) The book of Esther finds the Jews scattered all over pagan lands and threatened with extinction. Many Israelites wondered, *Is God still in control? Is He still active in the lives of His people, or has*

Ie finally abandoned Israel? The writer of the book of Esther does
is best to answer these questions for his generation.

a brief chronology of the book of Esther

Xerxes I (Ahasuerus) becomes king	486 BC
Xerxes holds his banquet, deposes Vashti (Esther 1:3)	483
Persia fights Greece and is defeated	482–479
Esther becomes queen (Esther 2:16-17)	December 479– January 478
Haman plots against the Jews (Esther 3:7)	April–May 474
Xerxes issues the edict against the Jews (Esther 3:12)	April 17, 474
Xerxes issues the edict to protect the Jews (Esther 8:9)	June 25, 474
The day of destruction (Esther 3:13; 8:12)	March 7, 473
The first Purim celebration (Esther 9:17-19)	March 8–9, 473

spread out like butter

Remember how God told Israel that if they obeyed Him, He'd bless
hem and if they were disloyal, He'd send them back into exile? As
ve know, the Israelites rebelled despite the clear warnings God
gave them through His prophets. Being the God who sticks to His
word, He allowed Assyria to destroy and deport the northern tribes
of Israel in 722 BC. The southern tribe of Judah was spared that
ime, and the people concluded that they were invincible because
God was protecting them. So they just kept on happily sinning until
God did the unthinkable: He let Babylon smash Jerusalem (the city
where the temple was located) and exile the people of Judah.

So it went that the empire of Babylon ruled over Jerusalem for the promised seventy years (see Jeremiah 25:11-12). Then, as prophesied, Cyrus of Persia defeated Babylon in 539 BC (thereby inheriting the people of Judah) and instituted a new policy for his subjects: Deported peoples could return to their native lands and rebuild temples to worship their gods as long as they remained loyal to Persia, paid their taxes, and offered prayers for Cyrus. This meant that the Jews were finally free to return to Judah.

Like a caged prisoner that is finally freed, many of the Jews stayed in Babylonia, Persia, and Egypt because they were too afraid of the journey back to Judah. The weather was unpredictable and the neighbors potentially hostile, practically guaranteeing that the Jews would experience poverty and hardship. So although about fifty thousand Jews actually did return to Judah, as many as ten times that number stayed in exile.

the skinny on Xerxes

Xerxes is the Greek equivalent of the Persian name *Khshayarshan*. The book of Esther calls him *Ahasuerus*, which is the Hebrew version of the name. Because the NIV uses the Greek form, we'll use it in this study as well. In English, this name is pronounced "Zerk-seez."

The Greek historian Herodotus, who was born around the same time as Xerxes, wrote a book about the wars between Greece and Persia; he devoted a third of it to the reign of Xerxes. Herodotus described Xerxes as bold, ambitious, dangerous, handsome, stately, and self-indulgent. He was also a seducer of women, whether it be his own wife or someone else's. In fact, he seduced both his brother's and his son's wife. Lots of family disputes resulted, and Xerxes actually had his own brother and nephews killed, along with their entire army.

Saying Xerxes was a bad guy is really an understatement. We tend to be shocked by the Saddam Husseins of the world as if they're rare, but Saddam-like behavior was standard fare for rulers in

Esther's time. Esther knew her husband was like that, and though she wasn't shocked by him, she was terrified of him—and with good reason. Even Herodotus thought Xerxes' behavior was a bit much by Greek standards.

about the book

Although Esther is found in the first half of the Old Testament, it was actually one of the last to be written. Its author is unknown, but he was almost certainly a Jew living in the Persian Empire, perhaps in Susa. Scholars have concluded this because the author had accurate knowledge of Persian customs and terms. His description of the citadel of Susa was precise. He probably wrote after Xerxes died in 465 BC when such an unflattering portrait of the king would not have endangered Mordecai and Esther or himself. It is also likely that he wrote before Alexander the Great conquered the Persian Empire in 331 BC because he used Persian words frequently but never used Greek ones.

The author uses interesting writing techniques. For example, he duplicates some of his records: two lists of the king's servants (1:10,14), two reports that Esther concealed her identity (2:10,20), two gatherings of the women (2:8,19), two times when Mordecai is arrayed in royal robes (6:7-11; 8:15), two coverings of Haman's face (6:12; 7:8), and so on. See if you can identify other distinctive elements of the author's style as you read.

Some commentators call the book of Esther a "historical short story"; some say it's fiction. Others believe it's a wisdom tale written to illustrate the principles found in Proverbs.[1] It was probably also intended to be read liturgically (as a worship ritual) at celebrations of the Jewish feast of Purim, which commemorates the events in this book.

Most Christians don't know what the feast of Purim is, but it is a favorite among Jews. In late February or early March, Jewish families gather to feast, give gifts, celebrate, and read the book of Esther out loud. Because the Jews have continued to be persecuted right up through this century, they genuinely love the book of Esther.

Although Jews hold the book of Esther dear, Christians have never been quite sure what to do with it. Martin Luther even wished it didn't exist at all because he said it "Judaize[s] too much" and is full of "heathen perverseness."[2] But whether you agree with Luther or not, one thing we know for sure is that standing up for who you are, where you come from, and the faith you claim is not easy. It could mean life–or death.

telling stories

Lesson 6

I will go to the king, even
though it is against the law.
And if I perish, I perish.

Esther 4:16

There are some kinds of stories we just can't get enough of. Stories that feature scheming, murder, love, divorce, revenge, fear, desperation, or triumph attract people like reality television tryouts attract sociopaths. The secret is, these kinds of stories aren't only found in outrageous, R-rated movies or books—you can find them in the Bible too. Esther's story would fit neatly next to any Harlequin romance or suspense novel. Esther is not your basic, everyday, ordinary, run-of-the-mill Sunday school Bible story.

And yet for Jews (and really, for most Bible lovers), Esther is a beloved story. Here's a story of a woman who was abducted from her family to become one of the king's many wives. She lived in a harem, which meant a lifetime of cattiness, gossip, envy, and hate. (It also meant her probability of happiness and parenthood was slim to none.) Esther's future in a word: hopeless. Her entire race was at stake—on the verge of complete annihilation—all because of an evil man's pride. But regardless of the stakes, she chanced her life, her only remaining asset. Esther's bravery and love for her nation make this a favorite book of the Old Testament.

Read the book of Esther.

1   As you read, observe the plot, the characters, any events or ideas that recur, and the spiritual content. Record any observations you have, but don't let taking notes get in the way of enjoying the book's drama, humor, and suspense.

Plot

Characters

Recurring events or ideas

Spiritual content

2   Look for references to God and religious acts (such as prayer and worship). What do you find?

3 Briefly describe your first impressions of the main characters:

Xerxes

Haman

Mordecai

Esther

4 What other first impressions or observations did you have?

5 In just a few words, describe what you think the book of Esther is all about.

6 What questions do you have about the story?

live

7 Does this story seem relevant to any areas of your life right now? How?

8 What theme of Esther had the most immediate impact on you? How can you apply this theme to your own life?

If you haven't already, read the introduction to Esther. Think about your place on the sticking-up-for-yourself scale and discuss how your personality affects the way you react to Esther's story. Does she inspire you? Scare you? Threaten you?

Then pray together, asking God to lead you through this second half of the study with an open heart and mind so you will be able to embrace this story and get to know God better.

go deeper

For further study, recall how often feasting and celebrating occur throughout the book. Give a verse reference and brief description for each feast, banquet, or celebration.

Then, notice the recurrence of fasting in the book. Note each time fasting is mentioned, who fasts, and why.

memory verse of the week

Did a particular verse make you think? Is there a verse you can't get out of your head? Write it down and memorize it. Allow God's Word to permanently brand itself in your head and your heart.

notes from group discussion

Xerxes: a husband and a king

Lesson 7

Then the king asked, "What is it, Queen Esther? What is your request? Even up to half the kingdom, it will be given you."

Esther 5:3

It's trendy for a woman to make a list of husbandly qualities she expects from her future spouse. You know, things like:

- Maturing Christian
- Good with children
- Affectionate
- Vibrant sense of humor
- Brown hair, blue eyes, tanned skin, perennial five o'clock shadow, six feet tall, uncanny sense of style, favorite color pink, wears Ralph Lauren cologne

After making a list like that, can you imagine marrying someone whose list more closely resembles this?

- King
- Polygamist
- Neglectful
- Murderous
- Loves alcohol and beauty more than intelligence

Esther, an average (albeit attractive) Jew living in Persia, didn't get quite what she had hoped for. And Xerxes, the king of Persia, got more than he bargained for. Review the book of Esther, paying special attention to Xerxes' character.

Review the book of Esther.

study

fyi

- *Citadel of Susa (1:2).* Xerxes' father, Darius, built Susa as a winter home. The citadel (aka capital or palace) was on a hill west of the city; it was both an impenetrable fortress 120 feet above the plain and a pleasure house for the court. Surrounding it was a river and a beautiful garden.[1]

- *White and blue (1:6).* White and blue-violet were the royal colors. The decorations in the garden of Susa were white and blue because it was used as a royal pavilion for parties (the pavilion has actually been found by archaeologists).[2]

- *To drink in his own way (1:8).* According to Persian law, every party guest was required to take a drink every time the king drank.[3] (How were the guests supposed to have a fluid conversation? So the other day . . . drink . . . as I was saying . . . drink . . . dang it!) Xerxes waived this rule because people were unable to keep up with him. The author of Esther points out how often Xerxes drank. And here's a bit of trivia: Did you know the Hebrew word for banquet is related to the word meaning *to drink?*[4]

- *Queen Vashti refused to come (1:12).* Vashti didn't give a reason for her refusal, maybe because any excuse would have been considered invalid. Some scholars have suggested that Xerxes asked her to come wearing only her crown (see 1:11).[5]

- *Wise men who understood the times (1:13).* The royal advisers were astrologers, experts in politics, and experts in Persian law. They had the rare privilege of talking with the king face-to-face.[6]

- *Virgins for the king (2:2).* The beauty contest described in 2:2-4, 8-14 was not one the girls hoped to win. Winners were guaranteed a life of frustrated isolation in the harem. They were unable to see their families, spent maybe one night of their entire lives with the king, never again saw another man (except eunuch servants), and likely never had children (which was extremely important for survival to the women of that time).[7]

1 Judging by the way Esther was written, it seems the author wanted his readers to evaluate the characters with Old Testament teachings in mind. How well did Xerxes measure up to the standards in the following passages from Proverbs?

Teaching in Proverbs	How Xerxes Measured Up
Proverbs 5:15-19; 31:3	Esther 2:1-4,12-14
Proverbs 31:4-9	Esther 1:10; 3:15; 5:6; 7:2
Proverbs 11:4	Esther 1:4
Proverbs 14:29	Esther 1:12,19-22; 7:7-10
Proverbs 16:12-13; 20:26,28; 29:12	Esther 3:8-11; 6:1-10; 7:3-10

2   Consider how Xerxes dealt with women: Vashti, Esther, and the virgins of his kingdom. What good or bad examples did he set for men (especially husbands)?

3   What do you think a godly woman should do if her husband gives a command like the one Xerxes gave to Vashti? Should her response be different if he gives her an indecent command (such as flaunting her naked body in front of him and all his friends)? Should a woman accept orders from her husband at all?

4   Who or what controlled Xerxes' life? Explain your answer with specific passages.

5   Are there any men in your life who remind you of Xerxes? If so, pray for them and ask God to help you forgive and love them. Read 1 Peter 2:13–3:6 and write down anything God may reveal to you.

live

6   Think about your own priorities, ways of dealing with people, and ways of making decisions. Are you like Xerxes in any good or bad ways? If so, how?

7   Based on your answer to the previous question, what does this study make you want to change about your habits, priorities, methods, or decisions? How can you begin this process?

connect

Have you made a list of characteristics you'd like to see in your future spouse? If so, discuss them with each other. If not, share your initial thoughts about this. Pray over each other's lists, asking God to provide you with a spouse who fits His criteria (which may or may not be your own). Ask God to begin preparing your heart to be a loving marriage partner if that is the life He is calling you to.

go deeper

Spend more time considering question 3. Read the following verses and answer this question: What should a Christian do if she finds herself married to or working for a man who shows traits like Xerxes? (Even if you're not married, think hard about this question. It may help you make decisions in your dating relationships now that will impact your future.)

- Luke 6:27-42
- Romans 12:17-21; 14:1-23
- 2 Timothy 2:22-26
- Hebrews 10:23-25; 13:4
- James 3:13-18
- 1 Peter 2:1,18-25; 3:1-22; 4:12-16; 5:6-11

memory verse of the week

Did a particular verse make you think? Is there a verse you can't get out of your head? Write it down and memorize it. Allow God's Word to permanently brand itself in your head and your heart.

notes from group discussion

Mordecai and Haman: trading spaces

Lesson 8

So Haman . . . robed Mordecai, and led him on horseback through the city streets, proclaiming before him, "This is what is done for the man the king delights to honor!"

Esther 6:11

You know how Jesus said, "The last will be first, and the first will be last" (Matthew 20:16)? Well, it seems the idea was true even before He came to earth. Mordecai and Haman, two very different men, demonstrate that truth better than most. Yet, interestingly enough, the two of them had some things in common.

Both Haman and Mordecai knew they were not in total control of their lives. They also knew they had a destiny to fulfill. Yet while one man fought (to the death) to keep himself, his stately position, and his racist agenda alive, another saved the king, humbled himself, and did everything he could to save his entire nation. For all Haman cared, anyone who got in his way could die. Actually, he believed it'd be best if *all* the Jews died. Mordecai's humility and service, on the other hand, lifted him up to the highest post in the empire.

Review the book of Esther.

fyi

- *Jew of the tribe of Benjamin (2:5).* The term Jew technically referred to a man from Judah, but after the exile it was applied to Israelites of all tribes. Jair, Shimei, and Kish were probably not Mordecai's immediate ancestors; Mordecai was too young to be the great-grandson of Kish, who was exiled in 597 BC. It's more likely that the verse names Mordecai's prominent ancestors, which was a common thing to do in ancient genealogies. These names show that Mordecai was of King Saul's family and probably from one of the noble houses of Judah.[1]

- *Sitting at the king's gate (2:19).* The king's gate was the entrance to his palace (similar to what you read about in Ruth 4:1-11). The king's officials hung out at the gate and helped people seeking justice. When Esther became queen, she apparently made sure Mordecai was appointed as a judge (which wasn't a great position in the Persian hierarchy).

- *Agagite (3:1).* It figures that Haman, stuck up as he was, was no more Persian than Mordecai. He descended from Agag, king of Amalek. Israel had been perpetually at war with Amalek ever since Amalek attacked Israel after the Exodus. Israel was supposed to have killed every Amalekite and destroyed all their property. But King Saul's army wanted to keep the plunder instead of burning it, and so he gave in to them, sparing the life of King Agag against God's orders. It's significant that five hundred years later, a descendant of Saul confronted a descendant of Agag, giving the family a second chance to obey the Lord. This ancestral feud obviously helps us understand why Haman was so adamant about killing off the Jews, and it helps explain why Mordecai refused to obey Haman.

- *Ten thousand talents (3:9)*. The annual income of the Persian Empire was about fifteen thousand talents, so Haman was offering two-thirds of that amount—obviously, a huge sum.

- *Tore his clothes . . . sackcloth and ashes . . . wailing (4:1)*. These were common signs of grief in the ancient world. Back then, expressing emotions was more dramatic than we often see among modern westerners. Mourning and fasting in those situations was almost always accompanied by prayer, so it seems the author deliberately didn't mention God.[2]

- *One of the king's eunuchs (4:5)*. Mordecai and Esther had to talk to each other through a eunuch because Esther couldn't leave the harem and Mordecai couldn't enter the citadel in mourning clothes.

1 On one level, the book of Esther shows a clash between two very different men. What do you learn about Haman from these passages?

3:1-15

5:9-14

6:4-14

7:6-8

2   How did Haman's life exemplify Proverbs 3:33-35; 6:16-19; 11:2; 14:22; 16:5,18?

3   Now describe Mordecai's personality and ethics according to these passages in the book of Esther:

2:19-23

3:1-4

4:1-17

5:9

8:1-2,9-10,15

9:20

9:4; 10:3

4 On a deeper level, the story depicts a conflict between two views of how the world works.

> **a** In Haman's view, what controls history and life? How did this affect the way he lived?

> **b** And in Mordecai's view? How did he live according to his beliefs (passively or actively)?

5   After reading Esther 2:21-22; 3:2-4; and 5:9, what do you think you would have done in Mordecai's place? What about in Haman's place? Can you relate to either of them?

live

6   Mordecai was the person who convinced Esther to act on behalf of the Jews. Why do you think she obeyed him?

7   How can you influence others the way Mordecai did?

connect

Do you think you have a destiny? If so, who or what determined that destiny, and who or what will make it happen? If not, why not? In your groups, think about this question in light of the book of Esther. Discuss your thoughts with each other.

go deeper

Compare Mordecai to Boaz. What traits do they share, and how do they differ?

memory verse of the week

Did a particular verse make you think? Is there a verse you can't get out of your head? Write it down and memorize it. Allow God's Word to permanently brand itself in your head and your heart.

notes from group discussion

Esther: from the harem to the history books

If I have found favor with you, O king, . . . grant me my life — this is my petition. And spare my people —this is my request.

Esther 7:3

Imagine you're going to a political convention where there's a powerful, slimy, crooked politician on stage. You are not a reporter or anyone who matters at all to the politician. But you have something to say, something very important to you, and you know he probably won't respond well. Imagine that you somehow sneak your way into the convention, uninvited, and gather the guts to express your thoughts to him. Odds are that success is unlikely. Not only that, but you're putting yourself at risk.

On a more deadly scale, the odds that Esther would have a successful encounter with Xerxes were just as impossible. But there was something extremely unique about her—she emerged from the crowds of a royal harem, a place where she was just as obscure to the king as his gardener, to become King Xerxes' favorite wife (at least for a while). She rose above the great probability of death to save an entire race—one that raised up the King of kings.

Review the book of Esther.

- *Hadassah . . . Esther (2:7)*. The Hebrew name Hadassah means "myrtle," a plant that for the Jews symbolized peace with God and prosperity (see Isaiah 41:19; 55:13). The Persian name Esther means "star"; it sounds like Hadassah and suggests the star-shaped myrtle flowers.[1]

- *Favor (2:9,17)*. The Hebrew word for this, *hesed*, is used often in Esther (and in Ruth). It normally is used for God's covenant love. Jewish readers would recognize the word hesed as a very deliberate mention of God (without overtly mentioning God).

- *Without being summoned (4:11)*. It's not clear why Esther didn't just request a meeting with the king instead of going to the throne room unannounced. Maybe she expected a long delay before she could get an appointment (just imagine having to set an appointment with your "other half"), especially because Xerxes hadn't asked to see her in over a month. Visiting without summons was, for many reasons, a dangerous move—partly because she was isolated in the harem and had no idea what political concerns the king had, what kind of mood he was in, or which wife he currently favored.

- *Banquet (5:4)*. No matter what the time, the king and queen were never alone in the throne room. There were inevitably retainers, guards, officials, and sometimes foreigners there for state business. Esther wisely planned to make her request in a more private, less formal setting—a banquet—where the public would not observe the king change his mind about a law he'd made just because his wife influenced him.[2]

1 What do you learn about Esther from these verses: 2:7,9,10,15,17,20?

2 Why was Esther reluctant to approach her husband for the sake of saving her people?

3 Consider her final decision and her words to Mordecai. What does 4:12-16 tell you about Esther's character, priorities, and beliefs?

4 Why do you think Esther wanted all the Jews in Susa to fast for three days with her (see 4:16)?

What does fasting signify? Do you think Christians should fast? If so, why? If not, why not? (Optional: See Isaiah 58:1-14; Matthew :16-18; 9:14-17; James 4:7-10.)

5   Esther probably asked Xerxes and Haman to the first banquet to avoid making her request public (see 5:4). Her reason for postponing heir second meeting is less obvious.

    a What did this second delay accomplish (see 5:9–6:14)?

    b Could Esther have foreseen these events? Why do you think she decided to wait another day?

7   What example(s) does Esther set that we should follow?

8 Mordecai saved his pagan king's life but refused to bow to Haman, his official supervisor. Esther broke the law by approaching the king without an appointment.

a Do you think they were generally obedient to the law and loyal to the king? Why or why not?

b Are there any lessons here for Christians living under non-Christian governments? What are they?

live

9 What can you do in your position or circumstance to help God accomplish His will according to His Word? What risks are involved? What help do you need?

10 How will you begin accomplishing the things you listed for the previous question?

connect

Think about Esther's character and decisions. Discuss together which you think are right and which you think are wrong. Then, talk about the way God chooses people to accomplish His work. Pray together, asking God to give each of you a purpose to further His kingdom.

go deeper

Esther hid her Jewish ethnicity for five years (see Esther 2:10,20). During that time, she didn't avoid "unclean" food, nor did she openly worship the God of Israel. As queen, she had to attend events in honor of Persian gods. Was she right or wrong in doing these things? Are there any circumstances in which it is right for a Christian to hide his or her faith in Christ? Under which circumstances is it *not* okay? What does the New Testament say about this?

memory verse of the week

Did a particular verse make you think? Is there a verse you can't get out of your head? Write it down and memorize it. Allow God's Word to permanently brand itself in your head and your heart.

notes from group discussion

the Lord of history

These days should be remembered and observed in every generation by every family, and in every province and in every city.

Esther 9:28

Sometimes a story is obviously about God, whether it actually speaks of Him or not. Consider C. S. Lewis's great work *The Chronicles of Narnia* or modern-day tales such as *Braveheart*. These tales never mention God, but seeing Him between the lines is easy. On the other hand, sometimes readers (or viewers, depending on the medium) have to work to understand the spiritual implications in a story.

If you were reading Esther in isolation rather than as a part of the Bible, you might not immediately notice God's involvement. The author of Esther must have had important reasons for never mentioning Him. Perhaps God also had a reason for leaving His name out of it. Maybe He wanted us to learn about Him through story, through experience. Whatever the reasons, let's take a look at the spiritual implications found in the story of Esther.

Review the book of Esther.

Skim through the book and write down at least six references to ucky" or "coincidental" occurrences. How might God have been volved behind the scenes?

2 Even though God, prayer, and worship are never mentioned, we now God wasn't absent. What role(s) do you think He played?

3 How does the book of Esther illustrate Proverbs 21:1?

4 Is this proverb applicable to your life in any way? If so, how?

5 Why was Mordecai certain that "deliverance for the Jews will arise" from somewhere (Esther 4:14)? Check Genesis 12:1-3 and Isaiah 41:8-16 to get some insight on this.

6 Many Jews had been defeated in battles and other catastrophes in the past, so Mordecai and Esther knew their survival was not guaranteed. Why did God permit defeats for the Jews but not total destruction (see Deuteronomy 4:25-32; Isaiah 54:4-10)?

7 Can Christians count on God's favor just like Mordecai did? Why or why not? See Romans 4:13-25 and Ephesians 2:11-22 for help. Knowing this, what should Christians expect from God?

8 Think about the stories of Ruth and Esther. Based on these books, what responsibility do we have in the fulfillment of God's plans?

What kinds of things does God do to make sure His plans work out?

10 What has God promised to accomplish in your life? What is your responsibility to help Him make those promises a reality? Consider the promises in Luke 21:10-19; John 15:1-17; and Acts 1:8

11 What else have you learned from this lesson that you can apply to your life?

connect

Discuss with your group how you've been able to follow the examples of Ruth, Boaz, Esther, and Mordecai. Talk about the difficulties and rewards you've experienced from what you've learned and done. Since this is the last lesson of this study, talk about any overarching lessons you've learned. Finally, spend time in prayer, thanking God for bringing you together as a group and asking Him to continue to teach you lessons from these two books of the Bible.

go deeper

Look over the notes you've taken in these lessons. What do they tell you about yourself? What commitments or plans did you stick with? What didn't you follow through on? Write an action plan to live out the lessons you've learned from Ruth and Esther during the next month.

memory verse of the week

Did a particular verse make you think? Is there a verse you can't get out of your head? Write it down and memorize it. Allow God's Word to permanently brand itself in your head and your heart.

notes from group discussion

study resources

It's true that studying the Bible can often lead you to answers for life's tough questions. But Bible study also prompts plenty of *new* questions. Perhaps you're intrigued by a passage and want to understand it better. Maybe you're stumped about what a particular verse or word means. Where do you go from here? Study resources can help. Research a verse's history, cultural context, and connotations. Look up unfamiliar words. Track down related Scripture passages elsewhere in the Bible. Study resources can help sharpen your knowledge of God's Word.

Below you'll find a selected bibliography of study resources. Use them to discover more, dig deeper, and ultimately grow closer to God.

a study resource collection

TH1NK REFERENCE COLLECTION: *The Bible: Think for Yourself About What's Inside; Theology: Think for Yourself About What You Believe; Worldviews: Think for Yourself About How We See God.* Colorado Springs, CO: NavPress, 2006.

historical and background sources

Carson, D. A., Douglas Moo, and Leon Morris. *An Introduction to the New Testament.* Grand Rapids, MI: Zondervan, 1992.

Provides an overview of the New Testament for students and teachers. Covers historical and biographical information and includes outlines and discussions of each book's theological importance.

Packer, James I., Merrill C. Tenney, and William White Jr. *The Bible Almanac.* Nashville: Nelson, 1980.

Contains information about people of the Bible and how they lived. Photos and illustrations help the characters come to life.

Tenney, Merrill C., *New Testament Survey.* Grand Rapids, MI: Eerdmans, 1985.

Analyzes social, political, cultural, economic, and religious backgrounds of each New Testament book.

concordances, dictionaries, and atlases

concordances

If you are studying a specific word and want to know where to find it in the Bible, use a concordance. A concordance lists every verse in the Bible in which that word shows up. An *exhaustive* concordance includes every word in a given translation (there are different concordances for different Bible translations), and an *abridged* or *complete* concordance leaves out some words, some occurrences of the words, or both. Multiple varieties exist, so choose for yourself which one you like best. *Strong's Exhaustive Concordance* and *Young's Analytical Concordance of the Bible* are the most popular.

bible dictionaries

Sometimes called a *Bible encyclopedia,* a Bible dictionary alphabetically lists articles about people, places, doctrines, important words, customs, and geography of the Bible. Here are a few to consider:

The New Strong's Expanded Dictionary of Bible Words. Nashville: Nelson, 2001.

Defines more than 14,000 words. In addition, it includes an index that gives meanings of the word in the original language.

Nelson's New Illustrated Bible Dictionary. Nashville: Nelson, 1996.
Includes over 500 photos, maps, and pronunciation guides.

The New Unger's Bible Dictionary. Wheaton, IL: Moody, 1988.

Displays pictures, maps, and illustrations. Clearly written, easy to understand, and compatible with most Bible translations.

ine's Expository Dictionary of New Testament Words. Peabody, MA: Hendrickson, 1993.

Lists major words and defines each New Testament Greek word.

ible atlases

e often skim over mentions of specific locations in the Bible, but cation is an important element to understanding the context of a assage. A Bible atlas can help you understand the geography in a ook of the Bible and how it may have affected the recorded events. ere are two good choices:

he Illustrated Bible Atlas. Grand Rapids, MI: Kregel, 1999.

Provides concise (and colorful) information on lands and cities where events took place. Includes historical notes.

he Carta Bible Atlas. Jerusalem: Carta, 2003.

Includes analytical notes on biblical events, military campaigns, travel routes, and archeological highlights, as well as indexes. A very popular atlas for students, scholars, and clergy.

or small-group leaders

you are the leader of a small group or would like to lead a small roup, these resources may help:

eyerlein, Ann. *Small Group Leaders' Handbook*. Downers Grove, IL: InterVarsity, 1995.

Teaches the biblical basis and growth stages of small groups. Helps leaders develop skills for resolving conflict, leading discussion, and planning for the future.

McBride, Neal F. *How to Lead Small Groups*. Colorado Springs, CO: NavPress, 1990.

> *Covers leadership skills for all kinds of small groups. Filled with step by-step guidance and practical exercises focusing on the most important aspects of small-group leadership.*

Polich, Laurie. Help! I'm a Small-Group Leader. Grand Rapids, MI: Zondervan, 1998.

> *Offers tips and solutions to help you nurture your small group and accomplish your goals. Suggests techniques and questions to use in many Bible study circumstances.*

bible study methods

Fee, Gordon, and Douglas Stuart. *How to Read the Bible for All Its Worth*. Grand Rapids, MI: Zondervan, 2003.

> *Offers chapters on interpreting and applying the different kinds of writing in the Bible: the Epistles, the Gospels, Old Testament Law, Old Testament narrative, the prophets, psalms, wisdom literature, and Revelation. Also includes suggestions for commentaries on each book of the Bible.*

LaHaye, Tim. *How to Study the Bible for Yourself*. Eugene, OR: Harvest House, 1998.

> *Teaches how to illuminate Scripture through study. Gives methods for understanding the Bible's major principles, promises, commands, key verses, and themes.*

Wald, Oletta. *The New Joy of Discovery in Bible Study*. Minneapolis: Augsburg, 2002.

> *Helps students of Scripture discover how to observe all that is in a text, how to ask questions of a text, and how to use grammar and passage structure to see the writer's point. Teaches methods for independent Bible study.*

notes

Lesson 2: Questioning God

1. Leon Morris, *Ruth: An Introduction and Commentary* (Downers Grove, IL: InterVarsity, 1968), 246.
2. Morris, 248.
3. Morris, 249.
4. Roland de Vaux, *Ancient Israel: Volume 1: Social Institutions* (New York: McGraw-Hill, 1965), 39–41, 54; Morris, 255.
5. Morris, 250–253.

Lesson 3: Crazy Things

1. Kenneth Barker, ed., *The NIV Study Bible* (Grand Rapids, MI: Zondervan, 1985), 366.
2. Barker, ed., 366, 368; Leon Morris, *Ruth: An Introduction and Commentary* (Downers Grove, IL: InterVarsity, 1968), 285.
3. Morris, 286–287, 289; Barker, 368.

Lesson 4: Faithfulness Through Thick and Thin

1. Leon Morris, *Ruth: An Introduction and Commentary* (Downers Grove, IL: InterVarsity, 1968), 297–298.
2. Roland de Vaux, *Ancient Israel: Volume 1: Social Institutions* (New York: McGraw-Hill, 1965), 54.
3. Morris, 300–301.

Introduction to Esther

1. This study follows the scholars who believe Esther is historically accurate. If you'd like to learn more about the debate, you should consult commentaries for more information.
2. Martin Luther, *Table Talk*, 22; quoted in Joyce Baldwin, *Esther: An Introduction and Commentary* (Downers Grove, IL: InterVarsity, 1984), 52.

Lesson 7: Xerxes: A Husband and a King

1. Joyce Baldwin, "Esther," *The New Bible Commentary*: Revised, ed. Donald Guthrie, et al. (Grand Rapids, MI: Eerdmans, 1970), 413. (This book is not cited hereafter.)

2. Joyce Baldwin, *Esther: An Introduction and Commentary* (Downers Grove, IL: InterVarsity, 1984), 20. (This book is referred to hereafter as Baldwin.)
3. Baldwin, 58–59.
4. Baldwin, 56.
5. Baldwin, 60.
6. Kenneth Barker, ed., *The NIV Study Bible* (Grand Rapids, MI: Zondervan, 1985), 720; Baldwin, 61.
7. Baldwin, 67–68.

Lesson 8: Mordecai and Haman: Trading Spaces

1. Joyce Baldwin, *Esther: An Introduction and Commentary* (Downers Grove, IL: InterVarsity, 1984), 65; Kenneth Barker, ed., *The NIV Study Bible* (Grand Rapids, MI: Zondervan, 1985), 721.
2. Baldwin, 76–77.

Lesson 9: Esther: From the Harem to the History Books

1. Joyce Baldwin, *Esther: An Introduction and Commentary* (Downers Grove, IL: InterVarsity, 1984), 65–66.
2. Baldwin, 86.